A Slant of the Light

Latter-Day Poems

WARWICK McFADYEN

Title: A Slant of the Light
           (Latter-day Poems)
Author: Warwick McFadyen
ISBN: 978-0-646-73538-2

© Warwick McFadyen 2026
Copyright resides with the author.
The moral rights of the author have been asserted.

Previous titles:
The Life and Times of Mr Agio
The Ocean
21 + 4
Centre of Zero

Published by McFadyen Media
Cover photographs: Warwick McFadyen
Painting page iv: Hamish McFadyen

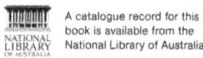
A catalogue record for this
book is available from the
National Library of Australia

CONTENTS

A Slant of the Light 1	The Fifth 29
Awakening 2	The Long Dry 31
Breath 3	The Rain Day 23
Breathless 4	The Voice 33
Cloud Fishing 6	The White Out 34
Clouds 7	To Speak of Silence 36
And Then 8	The Return 37
Counting Backwards 10	The Touch 39
January 26 12	Watching Trains 40
Marking the Page 13	The Stone and the Well 42
Lunar 15	Afternoon Storm 44
Power and Alienation 16	Pen and Hand 45
The Lost Children 18	Sunday Morning 46
Shade 20	Sculpt 47
Shoreline 21	Solstice 48
How to Speak to the Words 22	Flowers 49
Thoughts on the eve of Christmas 24	The Departed Earth 50
The Christmas Table 26	The Hours 51
Drinking Coffee 27	The World Below 52
The Distance of Three Stars 28	The Path 53
	The Equation 54

For Pip and Grace
and
without him, and within us,
Hamish

A Slant of the Light

A slant of the light
came visiting
upon the morning air.
I swam its streams
its mist-filled dreams,
inhaled the hour as prayer.

A breeze rose and sighed,
where you now look
may not tomorrow be,
the sway of light
is but time's kite;
sky tethered is not free.

Yet into the light
I kept my faith,
That even in shadows
falling I knew
its name as true:
love is the light I chose.

Awakening

Blur of shapes and colours shifting
greet new eyes in the first lifting
of lids raw to the world's glare
now washed clean of the womb's care.

Into the day uncomprehending
they open forever to the awakening
within them — the light and dark,
the silence, space, shadow and spark

the heartbeat of souls, the thread
of stars, the words said and unsaid.
In time, this is the sea floor deep
below the surface of all our sleep.

We are the world by senses made,
the notes on the wind played,
the distant call, the close breath
the fragile line of vision to death.

Breath

Take your time, breathe,
flick sand into the eye
of the storm,
fold the woes of the world
into a napkin then place it
on the table next to a
bowl of roses.

Take your time, breathe,
carry the crest of the moon
in your pocket,
run your fingers gently
along its arc of light
and feel not darkness
but the sky.

Take your time, breathe,
let the gales that travel
through hollow
bones, that howl to shape
another's soul pass through
you into dust and become
dead silence.

Take your time, breathe,
grasp the core of nothingness
in your hands
and give it meaning.
This will be your
defining moment.
Take your time, breathe.

Breathless

Breathe
in,
then
out.
Again.
In,
then
out.

Caress of air
upon the lips
ebb and flow
rise and fall
washing into
flesh and blood
washing into
signs of life.

Breathe
in,
then
out.
In,
then
out.

Into the world of
whirlwind,
of gasping terrors
and beauty,
of shoals of silence.

At the edge of an ocean,
rippled, crested,
formed, reformed
windblown, becalmed
is your voice.

This life will take
your breath away.

Breathe
in,
then
out.
In,
then
out.

Cloud Fishing

He cast his line into the air,
not to watch it fall
into the sea, but to see it
taken by the sky's call.

He was cloud fishing,
waiting on the feel
of a caught droplet
run down to the reel.

He needed no lure,
no bait on the hook;
he dreamt of the wisps
once river and brook

now blown by winds
into forms and
then unformed
unto ocean and land.

He cast his line into
the changing skies,
to catch a wisp of cloud
and hold it in his eyes.

Clouds

He looked at the clouds
and felt what he saw
untouchable
was him at his core.

We were both, he said
to the drifting sea,
a small part of the
other, me and thee.

Each drop of water
the arrival and
the leaving, the flux
of ocean and sand.

The clouds scudded by
and he heard at times
the singing of the
wind's ravelling chimes.

And then one droplet
fell from sky to heart
and the elements
flowed into one chart

that drew the nature
of life within him:
the cloud was his soul,
the sky was his hymn.

And then . . .

He was working
towards saying
everything
with no words.

How hard could it
be? Just replace
the nouns, verbs and
well, the letters

with the silence
of the distant
stars, with the sighs
of the soft breeze

with the murmur
of the surf's heart
with the night pull
of the moon's call.

with the wonder
he came to be
in the palm of
eternity.

Then he felt on
his lips the words
hope and love form
so soundlessly
and he knew that
everything
was enfolding
words and no words.

Counting Backwards

Counting backwards,
counting forwards
the heartbeats of the day
casting them to the air

see if they float
differently,
catching light and wind
holding my breath, not

holding my breath
for the seconds
to become sentences
for meaning to form.

Counting backwards,
counting forwards
the dark calculus
that shadows the eyes.

that turns on the
grains of blown sand
that speaks to the ash
surely, it can't be

this time for all
time — waiting for
a silence to break
that can't be broken.

Counting backwards,
counting forwards
forging days into
a chain of voices

that whispering
flow as a hand
moves, as eyes flicker
in the here and now.

These are the pale
numbers that add
and take the sum of
life from earth to sky.

Counting backwards,
counting forwards.

January 26

We used to call it the dead heart
as if nothing grew there,
as if nothing had ever grown
there, as if it was bare

of life, resident to mere rock
and dust, canvass of wind
dry-throated, unable to speak
so we did not listen

and lived by deafness and blindness
unknowing on the rim,
not of desert, but an ocean
of life in outstretched limb.

We live there still, at times reaching
into the heart, the beating heart
feel the pulse undying and ask,
whose was dead at the start?

Marking the Page

He began to write,
as the cliché would
say, his hand moved
the pen as it should.

It did not know its
course as much as he
tried to tell himself
they were one easy

stroke of communion
the thought and the deed
seamless like the root
stirring from the seed.

But each word contained
a galaxy deep
in stars and darkness;
awake and asleep,

spoken and silent,
and he yearned to hear
indefinable
notes of the spheres

that were life's rhythms
and he tried to mold
the sound to the soul,
as words he could hold
long enough to mark
on the page, to give
a faint, short voice to
the emptying drop.

Lunar

As the moon rose
so too the heart
its pool of light
the tidal chart

that places distance
from sky to earth
within the vault
that cradles birth

and draws each death
upon its walls
that says to each
this is your call.

As the moon rose
in passing phase
it winked just once,
these are your days.

Power and Alienation

The hollow man thought he had
power over everything,
a snap of the fingers
was the sound of a king.

I know what's best for you
and I know what's best for me,
when I speak the two are one,
this is the way of royalty.

The hollow man thought he had
by grace of god been saved
from the gun; to make the world
in his image was what he craved.

With a stroke of my pen,
with a word to my aide,
the blood will be drawn,
the price will be paid.

The hollow man thought he had
by his acts no one to answer to,
he saw vengeance as virtue
dealt out to those who not true.

The only reality I live in
is what I can buy.
My profit, your loss.
The only truth is the lie.

The hollow man thought he had
all nations in his hand,
to cower and kneel at his feet,
and give thanks to just stand.

I can seize your throat
I can enter your dreams,
I can sleep well at night
A conscience is not what it seems.

The hollow man thought he had
command over all, could school
choirs to stop singing; the
hollow man on the hill was a fool.

The Lost Children

Each time, the words
seem to fail us,
for what we've seen
for what we've heard.

You'd think something
would come to mind,
we asked our hearts
but no, nothing

has risen to
meet the silence
and sweep away
cruelty anew.

What then has come
again to us
to render the
senses as numb?

It is the sight
of a child, bone
pressing on skin
stone as to stone,

And a voice thin
of life and hope
trying to grasp
whatever sin

they must have done
to deliver
old death upon
them while so young.

And there are no
words of comfort
to give a child
dying fast and slow.

To bind war's aim
to clear conscience
collateral
damage we frame

it thus, and sigh
over the toll,
war is hell we
say, and so they

                die.

Shade

He sat on a park bench,
an oak tree stood nearby,
its long arms extended
to him a rustling sigh.

Take whatever you want
from me he thought he heard
it say: sorrow, laughter,
the lifesong of a bird.

The palms of my leaves can
cast the day into shade,
can shield your eyes to see
things in relief, not frayed.

He closed his eyes and then
reopened them. He felt
the light falling and for
just a moment he dwelt

among the pausing of
a world that was racing
before him, and drank in
the solitude embracing.

He sat on the park bench,
an oak tree stood nearby,
the earth waited for the leaf,
he held time with a sigh.

Shoreline

The blue waves broke
and ran rippling
on to the sand.
You are back
they murmured,
flowing through
outstretched hand.

I'd never left,
I replied, this too
was now my land,
this shoreline
these grains of
memory,
this sea strand.

This tide that held
in each moment
its own rise and
fall, that bore
wind and swell
as shadow,
as light bands.

They carry me
as I do them,
this is the flow
eternal
spring, mortal
heart, water's
edge. Stop. Go.

How to
Speak to the Words
Unwritten …

Try to grasp
the terrifying
tremelo
on the wind
- punch the air
slide your lips
along the clouds
stare not at the sun
but into it,
cradle the moon.

Try to shake
the sleeping
letters awake
that nestle,
like hatchlings,
in the branches
of the ghost trees.
Their slumber
is only the pause
in your heartbeat.

Try to gather
the sparks
of a fire
and its embers
in your hands
and frame them
both as the one
picture, then, you
will speak to the
words unwritten.

Thoughts on the eve of Christmas

He tries to measure
the distance of a bird
flying to the air
it flies through unheard

so high above him
silence, sky and wing
he thinks he cannot
grasp what they bring

to him, so far below
bound to the earth
his path footprints
strewn from birth.

Is it in the rising
and the falling;
is it in the heartbeat
of the wind calling

that pulls him towards
a space beyond reach
to swim in endless sea
without shore or beach.

This is the distance,
the long in longing
that is the breath of
love and belonging.

He knows then that
to hold love as the air
and bird hold each other
is the most sacred prayer.

The Christmas Table

There are places at the table
no more to be filled,
the knives, forks and plates
are not set; the glasses and cups
no more to be raised to lips.
They have been stilled.

Yet I see them on either side
of me, a father and a son,
both a part of my making,
both coursing through this day.
I am the midpoint in the journey
started and where it has run.

Their voices are not here, though
the air carries the lilt of the past.
When I raise my glass I hear a
murmuring on the rim: your
glass is not empty, it says, your
glass contains an ocean so vast

Sometimes the horizon cannot
be seen, for too deep is the sky
and its silence to grasp; drink
in the stars, swim the seasons
for on this day is borne the call.
Love, just love: for all that lives
                         must die.

Drinking Coffee

He raised the cup of coffee to
his waiting lips; it's black first thing
but he didn't need to say it
again, it was habit, a ring

worn on the finger day and night.
He took a sip, and let the steam
warm his face as it vanished
into the air, like shadowed dream.

He was no Prufrock measuring
out his life thus in coffee spoons;
distance was in the open palm,
in the glimmer of suns and moons.

In just a few more sips the cup
would be drained, the warmth now within
him, settling into his bloodstream
a murmuring of heart to skin

to last a little while day
flowed into night and grew chill,
until morning brought the next cup
to his lips, and he drank his fill.

The Distance of Three Stars

He supposed he could guess
the emptying distance
between the three stars,
flickering in the early
evening sky, growing
brighter as the day
seeps into the horizon
and darkness falls
like a beloved cliché.

He supposed he could guess
the distance of the
triangle of light
by stretching his arms
out; it would cover
the space well enough
to give the illusion of
what is far is near; that
earthbound is limitless

in the ways of the
imagination, that
we can throw ourselves
into the drifts of cloud
into the swirls of stardust
into the freefall of endless
possibilities that pulls us
to look into the galaxies
behind our eyes and see
the distance of three stars.

The Fifth

The full moon rolled
along the horizon
like a coin flicked
from the hand of
a cold, laughing god.

From the water's edge
he watched its rim
dissolve into
the wash, felt the swirl in
his open palms,

then cupped it as
a pool, cradling silence,
transformation,
the captured drops
of blood memory.

He waited then for
the sky to fold
in on itself
for the light to recast
its old canvas.

But the waves whispered:
what you gather
will gather you;
we are the surface wake
and the undertow.

From birth to last breath,
the moon was the
fifth, glissando
of notes rising, falling
now come to earth.

In the silence
he listened for a voice,
an echo of
the moon's shadow
to make a thin sound

like the brush of leaf
against the sky
like the murmur
of a heartbeat's rhythm
— the gentle swell.

Only now the
pulse of the stars
reached him, faint music
of a life — the interval
of the fifth.

The Long Dry

The grass has died
off, the green braid
now has been scythed
by summer's blade.

Pressed into dust,
cut from the sky
lifeless to those
who, passing by,

feel underfoot
the cracked dry stalk
from season drawn
brittle as chalk.

The grass that once
bent with the breeze,
that once grew on
the breath of trees

has died. Its roots
await the rains
and silence through
seasons remains.

The Rain Day

The day drew its grey shawl
over its shoulders bare
and whispered to him,
breathe in soft this air.

These drops have travelled
far from ocean to sky
their flow is the chain
we wear till last goodbye.

Life giving, death taking
compass of the heart,
geography of the soul
watermarks, fragile art.

He cupped his hands to
catch the drops as they fell,
of past, present and future,
this was the deep well.

The Voice

Each voice is a note
that plays on the air,
that floats on the breeze,
on the spray of seas.

Each voice is a note
that swells with love's calls,
that lifts souls sublime
but knows not its time.

Each voice is a note
that lightens the dark
that shadows the light
threading day and night.

Each voice is a note
that vibrates to stars
that gathers patience
from the earth's silence.

Each voice is a note
that sings of a life,
that carries a fire
- each voice is a choir.

The White Out

In and outside

the rhythm
of the seasons

the grass is white,
a stubble of life
that once was.

The birds say it is
the sky's dry breath
pressing against
the earth.

Their wings carry
the dust of its
indifference,
their feathers
streaked grey.

They scrape
against the thin air
where once
they would
have soared
among the clouds.

The rivers
are fingers
of bone,
splintering
from promises
of rain that
do not arrive.

The grass
can no longer
sing. It is white
as bone.
Its voice broken
on the rising
of the sun
and the wind.

He bends to the
earth and plucks
a strand of grass
and its roots,
plants them in
a sheltered pot,
gives them water.
And waits for the
greening to come.

To Speak of Silence

Let's pause, take this time
to speak of silence
when your words
without reliance

to the humming world
float in fractured air
when your words
wait for a breeze fair

to carry the sighs
of your calling heart
when your words
arrive and depart

to the sea's rhythm
to the storm's rage
when your words
describe the soul's page.

The Return

He was walking the hill
to his son's gravestone
his head was bowed
his eyes cast down
to count his steps;
how alike they were
to what a life
might be, he thought.

He could still go back
and yet not be there
he told himself,
the familiar
was still alive
among the contours
of light and shade
that brushed the stone.

But the maps were gone,
the charts faded grey
certainty now
just a sere leaf
brittle and cracked
on the dry earth where
he now stood and
looked to the sky.

What did he expect
in the returning,
voices unchanged
in the pitch and
toss of the breeze,
eyes blind to the roll
of the days down
the rutted roads?

And yet he returned,
to sit on the bench
beside a life
no more, to brush
away leaves from
his name, to rest from
taking a step
away from him.

The Touch

The hand on the shoulder
is both hello and goodbye
soft as an autumn sunset
gentle as whisper and sigh.

The waves of cusped light
it holds flow into my chest;
they nestle into the heart -
the leaving now always guest.

The hand on the shoulder
is both the warmth and the cold;
the stroke of time insistent,
seasons waiting to unfold.

It knits skin to memory
with threads of a distant star.
This is the tattoo I wear;
this is love, still, from afar.

Watching Trains

At the day's end
from platform five
watching the trains
depart and arrive

he stands back from
the edge, away
from the rails grind,
the steel and the grey

of lines worn smooth
by spark and glide
of wheels that feel
not the stop or ride.

Please stand behind
the yellow lines;
please, for safety's
sake obey the signs.

He knew the voices,
phrases that thread
the air each day
doors closing, he said

quietly, and
opening, to
no one and all;
train was coming through

stand back, for this
one did not stop
but sped past, a
ghost-laden teardrop

destination
unknown, blur
of the instant
a flash and a whirr

to him waiting
on platform five,
for his train to
depart and arrive.

The Stone and the Well

A stone sits
at the bottom
of a well.
It does not move.
Surface waves
do not reach it.
The wind cannot
brush against it.
Light filters
down, plays upon
the shoal of days
that is its bed.

He thinks to give
the stone a name,
for lack of
having a purpose.
He thinks though
it may be averse
to such things.
Perhaps a stone
at the bottom
of a well
is merely a
poem unread.

Or, perhaps,
too often read
by its silence
is given a
weight heavier
than words;
that turns it
into a stone
sitting at
the bottom
of a well,
immovable.

An Afternoon Storm in the New Year

Lightning cracked
the sky
sending shards
spinning,
like splinters
of wood
from an axe
singing.
Thunder poured
its growl,
snapped hard
its jaws,
bent the air
to say,
we are not
your laws.

Pen and Hand

He drew a line across the page,
it had no direction to it.
The pen had touched paper,
the hand had hesitated, then
began its flow of ink into
the centre of nothingness -
a universe waiting to be given
shape or meaning, or perhaps not.
Perhaps nothing could be read into it,
A line, merely a line, unspeaking and
undefined, just a mark travelling
until the hand stopped, and the pen
lifted off the page. Was this also his
signature, he thought? The page
fluttered in the flickering candlelight.
He held it down, and put pen
to paper a second time, and then a third.
Words formed where once was nothing:
My pen is my hand is my mark.
This is my signature, this is my universe.

Sunday Morning

How is his sleep -
do the ashes stir
in earth and on shelf?
If only dreams were

so alive to the heart
and could by footfall,
word and tear shape
an answer to the call.

He is not at rest. Nor
is restless, a flame
does not rise from
the ashes to claim

a new awakening,
yet on a Sunday morn
the living to the dead
kindle a light born

in another time and,
in the graveyard, place
it on the earthen bed
to warm his sleeping face.

Sculpt

How to shape beauty
from the ugliness
of the world,

How to work the cold
clay into magic
and soft light.

This he asked, as a
child to the full moon
might ask, why

do you not stay all
the time; not knowing
the turning

of the earth's axis
was the moon's giver
and taker.

He dipped his calloused
hands into the tides'
ebb and flow,

Breathed in, went to work.
Saw the heart's outline
awaiting.

Solstice

The calligraphy of the winter sky
writes in script drained of light,
it fills its canvass with the roar
of gales and the silence, white
and ocean deep, of the frozen shore.

He walks, as daydreaming, in the hours
of the dawn, its warmth now distant,
as a tide, a memory, that returns
on the waves, a flow of life extant
even on ice-laced air, that still burns.

Flowers

Still, the flowers grow among
shards of stone and memory.

Their rising into light is not
a promise given to us.

We gather colours from the fields
and give them meaning.

Pinned on lapels, placed on plaques,
arranged in vases and hearts.

They carry the seasons in their roots,
as do we, among stone and memory.

The Departed Earth

At sleep he saw
it still, the dawn
awakening
what was now gone:

Footprints on shore
returned to sand,
sigh of ripples,
a thinning strand

the fading breath
of ocean breeze,
the tide's final
grasp of the seas.

A gull alone
into this light
to the blue edge
faded in flight

pulled towards the
blurred line of sky
and the murmur
of winged goodbye.

This then was the
light in his eye
— time but a wick,
length of a sigh.

The Hours

The rain so soft
could not be seen
but in the nodding
of the leaves so green.

He knew its touch
faint in falling
whisper of water
to the earth calling.

These are the hours.
They play and drop
in the waiting air
giving life, then stop.

World Below

The smaller wheel
still turns.

The lesser light
still shines.

The weaker wind
still blows.

The gentler rain
still falls.

The fainter voice
still speaks.

This is the faith
that keeps

the heart ever
beating.

This is the pulse
hope undying.

This is the world
under the world

The Path

Walking the rising path
to the winter sun
the breeze catches
his bare-limbed thoughts
in early morning air.

He listens to the call
of birds, melodies
unchained to earth,
to build sweet song
as nests in the half light.

He holds a quivering
of time in open
hands, cradling it
from the shadows
crossing the narrow path

but with every step,
a part of it slips
away, falling
in the rising
like the lilt of bird song.

The Equation

By candlelight,
he considered
the equation

of the flame,
its flickering
and its shadows.

He took a pen
to paper
and wrote:

Each layer
of love
is the centre.

Each centre
of love
is a layer.

This is the
distance
without measure.

This is the
geography
of the heart.

This is the
axis and orbit
of star and moon.

Each layer
of love
is a grain.

Each centre
of love
is the shore.

www.ingramcontent.com/pod-product-compliance
Lightning Source LLC
Chambersburg PA
CBHW042226160426
42811CB00117B/1026